'A Diary of
Cottage l

G000129978

This is a personal journey and reminiscence of a job undertaken and completed through mine and my family's eyes. It's a journey of self-discovery and learning of new skills, the education of ones-self through success and mistakes and upon receiving general enlightenment and satisfaction of a job well done, from someone who had generally been working in an office up until this point.

Andy Rimmer

(Updated and revised edition February, 2022)

Third Edition ©Andy Rimmer, February, 2022

First Edition, (Blog version): 2010

Second Edition, (e-book): 2013

CONTENTS

A 'RE-INTRODUCTION'!

It has now been 15 years+ since we began this adventure; moving from England to Ireland, with the intent and ambition to reinvent ourselves and Marion's old family homestead in a rural Irish setting. To create a new business model that we would try and seek to match our new way of living and thinking and to then recognise how we could then leave a legacy to those that follow on behind us. In the intervening years a lot of things have changed, both globally, nationally and personally and also how we have viewed the progress we made with the cottage.

From the global aspect, rising temperatures and other weather phenomena's have reinforced our belief that our original 'eco' ideas were on the right path, if perhaps a little bit too early for many in this rural setting. The (inter)national changes came at exactly the wrong time for us personally, with the bank's / financial crisis leading to ditched or postponed ideas and plans. At times it felt like everything was being thrown at us, including the proverbial kitchen sink, but looking forward from early 2022 towards the future, we are still here, having learnt a host of new skills that at the outset we had no inkling of, matured, grown and gained new insight into our original ideas. From a personal viewpoint, our family has grown, developed and our daughter has now left for a new life at university. Priorities, like any parent will tell you, will change as circumstances change. The cottage has seen many adventures over this period of time as we now realise what we did right and what with hindsight can now be seen as honest but mistaken errors.

This revised edition of the original diary book will bring you the reader up-to-date with our adventures and point out where; in our thoughts we think we could have changed things for the better, in our own, personal grand design!

I hope you find the read interesting and fulfilling, whether you're using it as a point of reference, or just a quick curiosity read. Please always remember though, that this is just the personal recollections and observations of a personal journey of someone with no previous building experience, that we originally embarked upon in rural County Roscommon in mid-2006 and that every other potential renovation site or journey needs its own collection of expert advice, finance and enthusiasm in order to succeed.

"A Journey of a Thousand Miles Begins with a Single Step" (Chinese proverb)

Thanks for reading, Andy (November 2021)

Chapter One

Original Blog Date: Thursday, September 17, 2009

Connor's Cottage, Some History and a Personal Renovation Diary.

We are Marion and Andy Rimmer, and this is our personal diary, made from the various memories and notes scribbled down in notebooks and during the rather more calm, rational moments we had, covering and during our relocation from England to the West of Ireland in the summer of 2006; with the general intention of renovating Marion's derelict family homestead, in the beautiful and tranquil countryside outside of Roscommon Town and so to starting a new, exciting life with our young daughter in pastures new!

So, after the birth of our daughter in 2003, we as parents and individuals underwent a fundamental change of priorities and lifestyle. I had recently received a redundancy package from a large globally active international financial organisation, while Marion had decided to become 'a stay-at-home mum', which prompted the sale of our family home and in turn manifesting an observation of a positive change / re-awaking of our lifestyle and family values after a spell living in Uganda, East Africa and then returning to the UK. We had our moment of clarity, an epiphany or realisation that our lives were about to change forever. That present day, modern 'Western styled society' can be and often is a vast wasteful and polluting generation, that then led us to the decision that we should try and do our 'small' bit to help change things for the better. We had various options in mind, but eventually decided to move to the West of Ireland in June 2006, in order to renovate the old family stone cottage left derelict for over 30 plus years.

As can be imagined, some of our family and friends thought we were mad to even consider what we were planning to do, suggesting that we should just return to the humdrum ways of a regular job and commuter life before retiring to enjoy our later years in the usual accepted manner. But no, we stayed on course and here we are nearly 16 years later, still in Ireland but perhaps on a slightly different route to the one that we had originally planned. The way events progressed however, meant that we had the opportunity to build and develop our own business ideas off the back of the renovation project, which meant subtle re-thinks, tweaks and developments of business plans and the launch of a separate business diary blog, and in turn the publication of the first 'Kindle' edition of this diary.

To set the scene then, the original concept and thought behind our first and original 'Oceans Green Ltd' web site, (our registered company name once we landed in Ireland) was to document the history and the renovation of the family owned, but derelict, early twentieth century built Irish stone cottage, which had been left unoccupied for over thirty years since Marion's grandfather had died.

The cottage had seen a lot of activity over the years prior to it being left empty, with ten children being brought up in it, four boys and six girls. It wasn't the first building on the site though, the first cottage was closer to the barn and while excavating for the initial parking area we unearthed evidence of the stone hearth. But the existing building was subsequently built on higher ground, presumably to avoid damp and flooding and so Marion's grand parents moved into their new home and began a new exciting life and all that that entailed.

In the beginning! (The Summer of 2006).

As you might imagine, after being left empty and unused for over 30 years, the cottage was a bit of mess, (to put it mildly). It was overgrown; (see the pictures below) swallows and house martins had been nesting in the building; and even cattle from the neighbouring farm(s) had managed to get inside the building over the years. Add to this enough glass bottles scattered around the site from who knows where, with which we could have started our own recycling plant, (or so it seemed!)

The first step was to get a structural survey instigated to ensure that our plan was indeed possible and not just a pie in the sky illusion. It turned out that yes it was a viable operation, although the engineer did qualify his statement by saying most people would knock it down and start again; but because the building held so many memories for Marion, of old family holidays and her grandparents, we decided to proceed; and so, to action.

Our grand plan could continue and we could now look into how best to renovate, retaining or using as much of the old building and materials as was feasibly possible, together, of course, with the best of 21st century eco-friendly and sustainable technology that was available to us in the local area(s). We had made the decision to try and shop as local as possible, for as much of the renovation materials as we good, for the integrity of the project.

First off, to gain free access to the cottage, we had to cut back the overgrowth around the site, (which was about an acre in size all told, but only half of that immediately surrounding the cottage) and to start tidying the inside the cottage in order to ensure safe access to our building site. For this we had the help of Marion's brother Laurence and his family on their summer holiday!

One point that I haven't mentioned so far, was that the cottage is located at the end of single-track lane, a boreen to use the local description, with no drive or parking spot; we are surrounded by working farmland and cattle. So initially, in order to keep out of the way of the farmer(s) and their tractors we had to park on what would eventually be our garden area, but which had been regularly grazed on by the cattle, so not very flat or level! The only place that we could quickly and realistically place a proper parking / turning area in the lane was by the gate and next to the old barn, which was still in good condition thanks to Marion's uncle using it over the years to store various bits and pieces.

I thought the digging could be done fairly quickly by hand and shovel, (but welcome to Roscommon) it would have been, had it not been for the copious amount of large stone fragments and boulders found in the ground! However, on the bright side, it did give me a good supply of stone to begin re-building the dry-stone wall boundary surrounding the property.

Being rural, and in the west of Ireland, and having been derelict for over thirty years, I should also have mentioned that we had no running water or electricity on site. Prior to leaving England we had acquired an old French 'flat pack' caravan, that collapsed down into a trailer, but which afforded us a base camp to use whilst we were working on site, that was dry, somewhere to eat and sleep if necessary and was reasonably warm with the camping heaters we had bought separately. The old scout motto of 'Be Prepared' comes to mind!

The inside of the cottage preparatory work, meant the clearing of years of wildlife activity from the floor, walls and ceiling, before we then decided it would probably be a good idea to remove the low ceilings, (low so as to retain as much heat as possible in the old days, with no insulation in the original building) and broken windows, before one or both fell on top of someone and cut or injured them severely!

Having successfully completed this deep clean and safety sweep, we then had to make the cottage weather-proof for the winter of 2006/7; blocking up the windows and doors, then covering up the few missing roof tiles before settling back and planning the how, when and what to use in the coming new year.

Oh yes one other thing, before anything else, we had to remove the several large, well-established trees, bushes and roots that had grown quite voraciously over the years and close to the front door and walls of the cottage; at least it would provide fire wood later on!

The Planning & Sourcing of Materials Begins! (Early - 2007)

Over the winter, plans were made and then re-made. Research into sustainable energy and technology was undertaken, costings made and a way forward planned. It was decided that the original concrete roof tiles should be removed and replaced with natural slates, and as we were considering rain harvesting, we would incorporate a copper ridge system on the new roof, which would help to eliminate the growth of moss and other vegetation on the new roof. One of the two existing chimneys would be taken down below roof level and sealed off as we would not be using open fires in the cottage because of the waste of heat and energy straight up the chimney! Where the render on the outside walls and remaining chimney had become loose or already fallen off, we would replace and / or patch with a lime - hemp render, which as well as being old technology would significantly help the insulation properties of the cottage. Over this we would then place a weather-proof coating of sand-lime render, again old technology which would hopefully complement the stone construction of the cottage to the max.

We would source new double-glazed windows to the size of the existing openings, imitating the old sash windows if at all possible. Insulation would be extremely important, as we were planning to maximise the insulation properties at the expense of heating appliances, in fact we had decided early on that the only source of heat would be a solid fuel range in the central room of the cottage, (again keeping things as close to the old style interior as possible, but with a modern twist) as the room sizes were not that large and radiators would make a noticeable difference to space jutting out into the rooms, (some friends and family members did try pointing out that we were now in the West of Ireland, not Uganda at this point!) We eventually decided to use natural hemp insulation in the walls and roof together with 'Sasmox' boarding, with compatible wall membrane and vapour barrier to maximise the insulation barrier, inside a wooden 4inch stud.

As we had decided to try and be as self-sufficient as possible on the utilities front, we had to research and seek sources for power, water and sewage treatment. The water would be our first target once we had the cottage weather tight and we would resolve this by having arranging for a well drilling firm to visit the site at a later date; and to our surprise the sight of a genuine water diviner going around the property with his divining rods and confirming the presence of an underground stream going through the property and relatively close by to the cottage, before we then okayed the boring of our own well, (which struck water about a hundred feet down underground) to the rear of the cottage.

We had also decided on the buying of a compost toilet, (from Canada on-line as it happens, as no-one had yet entered into that particular market in Ireland, or were very good at advertising!) In turn this thereby removed the need for us to find a separate way for us to 'treat any black water', or sewage on site; while the remaining 'grey water' or soapy, washing water would be dealt with in a specially dug 'soak away' or 'reed bed' system. In fact, the advertising stated that when emptying the toilet of its 'solids', all you needed was a rose bush or flower bed!

Electricity had been connected to the cottage previously but was now obviously long since cut-off and while initially our needs were covered by a petrol run generator, it wasn't the cheapest way to provide us with electricity; we had decided that it should be a sustainable source of power that we integrated into our development plans and eventually be generated from a small wind turbine, or wind / solar combo system, the brand and origin still to be decided upon with cost a serious factor, as initial searches had showed a significant difference in providing similar sized equipment.

TO BE CONTINUED.

Chapter Two

Original Blog Date: Thursday, October 1, 2009

The Renovation Continues – 'And So To Work!' (2007 Through To Early 2008).

By late spring / early summer, material orders were being made to actually start the renovation project. Laurence, (an electrician by trade and also having had previous experience of a sustainable new build project) had returned to help out over the Summer, joined later by his son Laurence jnr. An Irish cousin of Marion's, Sean (a roofer by trade) was roped in to help with the roof work, so we were lucky in being able to utilise family skills to help renovate the old family home! We had ordered the natural slates and a copper ridge system for the roof; new double glazed windows and external doors, that imitated the original sash windows, with argon gas filled voids to maximise the insulation effect; we had also ordered the insulation materials, hemp and 'Sasmox' boarding, together with the lime / hemp and sand / lime which as well as acting as a plaster / render material, acts as a heat store and therefore, again acts in an insulation manner.

The old roof tiles were removed, a major task in itself, as a great deal of copper wire had been used in the original building operation to tie the tiles onto the wooden joists. At this stage we found the roof wood was actually in very good condition considering how long the building had been empty, we only had to replace or strengthen a few pieces of the existing wood. At this stage, we also treated the roof timbers with an eco-friendly insect / preservative treatment.

With the tiles finally removed, we could also begin to take down one of the chimneys below roof level and seal it off; its construction, like the rest of the cottage was of outstanding quality and took us rather longer than planned to finish. Thereafter, we began laying the new roofing felt and slates. We got lucky with the weather as well! Sun instead of the traditional Irish wind and rain and with Sean's assistance good progress was made on the roof in a timely manner.

A curious aspect of the cottage was the placement of the porch, (from one brought up in 'commuter belt' southern England) which had been built inside the cottage front door - in the main living room. It was something we wondered about from time to time, but as summer moved into autumn and the wind and rain became more constant, we realised that it was probably how the family got quickly out of the rain when coming home in the past. Anyway, the solid stone built internal porch in the living room had to go, obviously it was taking up much needed room inside the cottage, but also because the windows and external doors were being delivered and we didn't want to risk breaking any of the glass in them. A strange observation note at this point; we had wanted to get wooden frame windows to imitate the original cottage windows, but when we saw the various samples from the glazers, the wood frames looked more like plastic and the UPVC frames looked more like wood; a strange world we live in!

Having got the windows delivered, we then got to work fitting them and the doors in accordance with the supplied instructions, (as we tried to save money wherever possible by doing the labour ourselves) but had to get a service engineer out to have a few adjustments made to the modern tilt and turn opening mechanisms.

The roof was now the main priority in order to complete making the cottage weather tight again, together with the repairs to the one remaining chimney. The chimney was sealed with the lime / hemp mix and as the slates were laid around the chimney, we inserted the copper flashing around its base (part of the copper ridge system). With the slates laid, the rest of the copper ridge system was put in place.

While the weather remained fine; hot, blue skies, big sun etc. we realised, (as briefly mentioned previously) that being an old property we had no running water on site. In the old days, the family used to head up the lane to a natural spring, or out into one of the fields to a stream and bring back buckets of water to the cottage, (much the same as still happens in Africa today). So, we decided to see if we could sink a well somewhere on the property. We contacted our well man, (Alan Dunne – Water Well Drilling) who came out to the property and began water divining around the grounds and within five minutes had found three or four strong positive sites for water. The deal was done and we waited for Alan to arrive with his drilling equipment the following day.

The next day we were on the roof when we heard what sounded like the biggest vehicle in the country coming down our tiny, whitethorn hedge enclosed lane. Sure enough, what looked like a launching vehicle for 'Thunderbird 3', (for those of you old enough to remember the TV series) appeared around the corner and pulled up at the gate.

Eventually, after packing the gate area with stone to help absorb the weight of the truck, Alan got the rig into position and began drilling and after what seemed like no time at all, we struck water, about 100 feet down. The bore hole was lined and we waited for the next part of the operation to happen. A couple of days later, we had the pump arrive and fitted and we could finally say that we had running water on site, (even if it was still temporally powered by a generator).

With the cottage weather proofed with a new roof and windows and doors, the next part of the operation was to begin work on the insulation inside the house. As previously mentioned, our aim was to maximise the insulation of the building as heating would be restricted to a solid fuel range and to one radiator, a heated towel radiator in the shower come wet room. At this stage, Laurence being an electrician by trade began putting the first fix wiring in place for later completion.

First of all, a wall membrane was fixed onto the internal stone walls and then a 4inch wood stud was built inside the cottage. Once the stud was in place and a smaller frame built around each of the windows, the hemp insulation could be fitted and then covered with the vapour barrier. As we were attempting to maximise the insulation capabilities, it would not do to just put in the hemp and barriers before boarding over with the 'Sasmox' boards, we would have to use the associated glue and sticky tape to ensure all overlapping barriers were airtight. Thereafter, the 'Sasmox' boarding had to be fitted in place on the walls and the ceiling. The boards were a standard 8ft x 4ft, but because of their composition enhancing their insulation, soundproofing and fire resistance capabilities, they were somewhat heavier than normal plaster boarding. The boards could be put up on the walls in one piece, but the ceiling boards needed to be cut into smaller pieces, i.e. normally half or a third of the full size. Even then, the ceiling boards sometimes took two of us to position and screw into place. The next step in the process was to fill the gaps and board edges with 'Sasmox' filler, which was allowed to dry, before being sanded down to a smooth finish, ready to be painted with a natural paint in due course.

After a few delays and just before Christmas, we finally got delivery of our solid fuel range - although typically it wasn't as straight forward as you would expect by now. It was delivered on the back of a lorry and lifted off with the lorry's crane into the front garden and left there. Nowhere near the front door! The delivery driver was actually on his own in the truck with no assistance and said that he had no means to move the iron stove for us and said that that was what was on the delivery docket. We had no option but to rush up to the shop and shall we say, 'quietly' negotiate with the shop owner in front of several amused shoppers to actually get help in moving the range from in the front garden into the cottage as had previously been arranged when we ordered it!

Anyway, we finally had our source of heat and hot water. Now we approached another of Marion's cousin's - Enda, who is a qualified electrician and plumber, to help with plumbing in the range and helping to sort out the cottage plumbing in general and also second fix the electrical wiring.

What a great help it is to having so many qualified tradesmen in the family!

TO BE CONTINUED.

Chapter Three

Original Blog Date: Thursday, October 22, 2009

Into 2008 – The Renovation Continues.

Through the early months of 2008, the plumbing was sorted, with new holes being drilled & old ones filled.

A new chimney lining for the solid fuel range was put down the sole remaining chimney and secured, the pipework gradually fitted and connected around the cottage. Typically, the chimney vent for the new range was on the opposite side to the existing hole in the wall from the original range, (which we had found dumped outside the back door when we had first started the clean-up) and so we had to fill and block the existing vent and cut a new one through the stone work – not an easy job. As the range would also supply us with all of our hot water, all the pipe work had to work on a gravity basis, (although later on a small pump was added to help push the hot water around the system) which meant additional stone cutting to get the correct angles, before finally sealing and lagging the pipe work and filling the water tanks.

With the plumbing and pipework virtually complete, that just left the piping to take the grey water away from the cottage to the 'Soak' at the bottom of the garden, behind the original concrete chicken and pig sty/shed. As mentioned above, water movement on site was all designed to work through the force of gravity; the waste water was no exception. So, not having learnt my lesson from previous excavations with a shovel, I set about digging a trench from the cottage to the soak, about a hundred feet away, using gravity to move the water. Let's just say I didn't need to bother going to a gym while all this was going on! Anyway a few days later the pipework was laid, connected to the cottage kitchen and shower/wet room and the trench refilled and water was flowing into the soak. We had also decided to plant native willow shrubs around the soak rather than use reeds, to help the return to nature journey of the used grey water.

With the pipe work in place and with no supplier conveniently nearby, we had an opportunity to explore further afield and a trip to Dublin was next on the cards in order to find a traditional Belfast sink, period taps, shower fittings and basin for the kitchen and shower/wet room.

The one 'false wall' we had planned and eventually had in the whole building, had to be erected in order to help create the shower/wet room and incorporate the pipe work for the shower itself. Before long it was all in place and the shower/wet room lined and tiled throughout.

The compost toilet, (which now looked a lot bigger than we had originally thought, when we had bought it all those months previously) was installed. With the toilet in place, the floor tiling throughout the rest of the cottage could be laid, with a pattern flowing through the cottage from one room to another. The shower area obviously had non-slip tiles on the floor and bathroom tiles on all the walls and ceilings.

Once the tiling had been completed and grouted, (waterproofed where necessary) the toilet could be fixed in place and the integral toilet vent sealed in place through the roof, to help the evaporation / decay process and removal of any odours to the outside from the toilet itself. The final insulation was put into the ceiling area above the bedrooms at this point to finalise the insulation process and an access hatch to the loft area made and fitted.

At this point you might be asking what had happened to our source of power. We had been making do with a petrol generator, hoping to have in place a wind turbine / 'solar p.v.' combo unit; when we were ready to move in and test run the property, as suitable for human occupation again.

Well, we lurched from one problem to another, to disaster. From salesmen who were obviously not interested in selling to small time individuals and therefore priced their equipment accordingly, to those who would do anything and say anything to get a sale! We've spoken to them all, or so it seems!

Whenever we thought we had found a possible supplier, something would go wrong. In one case and following through on our intention to buy locally wherever possible, we were promised delivery on date after date, but nothing arrived. We had built a battery shed in accordance with the instructions received, ready for our battery bank; dug out by hand and filled in with concrete & reinforcing bars, a base area for the turbine pylon, (only to be told by another supplier's Rep. that our measurements were all wrong and that the turbine would probably fall over with the first big gust of wind to encounter it! The hole we had dug was like a cube, but should have been much larger in area and not so deep!

It was all pointless and frustrating in 2008 Ireland, as nothing arrived, or looked like arriving!

Eventually, we received a partial delivery of a turbine, batteries & solar panels. BUT, nothing to put the pylon on, no tower, framework or cabling, or even any instructions on connecting or setting anything up!

After numerous and persistent phone calls, e-mails and a visit to the company's office, we had to resort to threats of contacting the press, Government Minister's and various 'sustainable' organisations such as 'Sustainable Energy Ireland' (SEI) before we grudgingly got a refund! Even then, the company wanted to retrieve the equipment and inspect it at their factory before making the refund by cheque, which we quickly quashed as all the equipment was still in its original boxes and wrapping!

A point of note for those of you interested, we found out from a disgruntled employee of this particular firm, that the turbine we had had delivered, was actually a test turbine from the red stripe markings we saw on the blades and so just added more weight to our argument, that the owner of this firm had no intention of selling to us and just wanted the use of our cash for whatever reason!

Unfortunately, because of the actions of one, we now feel somewhat let down by this developing industry as a whole, almost as if they are already chasing the next big thing; watching their branches grow before the roots have given them a substantial base with which to take the weight above - and not even acknowledge the existing or potential new small time customers!

Anyway, after all of this turmoil, we eventually decided to bite the bullet and get connected to the grid for the time being, although we did go with 'Airtricity' to at least appear to be keeping the 'green' theme as far as possible.

The intention now, is to investigate further and maybe try and build our own wind turbine in the not-too-distant future, unless we find something more accommodating.

TO BE CONTINUED.

Chapter Four

Original Blog Date: Monday, November 9, 2009

Life Returns To The Old Cottage (2008 – 2009); MOVING IN – April 2008.

We have now decided that it was time to test our 'madness!'

So the three of us have now moved into the renovated, but as yet undecorated cottage, in order to make sure that everything worked and that our theory that maximising the insulation over heat sources was sound. So for the next nine or ten months, a family actually lived in the traditional, Irish stone cottage once again, for the first time in over thirty years.

The first observation of our stay was that a stone cottage left empty and derelict for any significant period of time, does need time to heat up and dry out! For perhaps the first three or four weeks of our time in the cottage, we awoke to condensation every morning on the floor tiles and windows as the building acclimatised to occupation again; my thoughts verging on frustration and helplessness as I allowed of all manner of negative emotions to rampage through my mind. However, slowly but surely as the cottage began to dry out, we and our lives took on new meaning and we began to start enjoying our new life in this renovated stone cottage.

Having our own water supply from the well is great from the financial perspective, once the initial drilling costs are paid back it's free water. However, it would be wise to arrange for a water test to see if there are any contaminants in the water and of course there is no fluoride in the water. The area we are in is for starters a hard water area, with a lot of lime scale. Also being a farming community you're never too sure what has been working its way back into the ground and water supply. After our test came back, we saw that we had high levels of iron in the water, so we invested in a suitable water filter for our drinking water.

We were able to celebrate Christmas in the cottage and lived through the best and the worst that the Irish weather could throw at us; we were as warm as toast inside when it was cold outside, (in fact having the windows wide open on Christmas day as the insulation was working so well) and nice and cool when it was hot outside. (It does get hot here sometimes!)

The range performed magnificently, cooking our food, heating us and the cottage and also warming our water, in fact sometimes we had to run off piping hot water as the circulating water couldn't cool enough by the time it got back to the hot tank. It also has to be said, that the flavour of our food off the range was so much better than virtually anything else we had previously experienced from gas or electric ovens!

We listened to and watched nature all around us, observed some spectacular sunrises and sunsets, even watching shooting star shows in the skies above, in the star infested heavens. There is definitely something to be said for living in the countryside away from neighbours and buildings and light pollution. We have also had family stay with us, to give us more of a feeling of how earlier generations may have lived together in the cottage, so closely in larger families and smaller buildings, than is generally the case today.

FEBRUARY – AUGUST 2009.

Having now proved to ourselves that the cottage was comfortable and habitable again, we moved out, in order to finish off the small things you can't do whilst living in a property like this. This is a cottage that does not immediately go hand in hand with twenty first century living; in today's world you are seemingly always growing with the number and size of possessions, whilst the cottage is compact and ideal for relaxing holiday breaks and weekend retreats. We could now finally decorate the inside of the cottage. The remaining large trees to the front of the grounds were taken down, saving the wood to season and burn in the range next year. By removing these tree's, we could now properly assess how much of the boundary walling needed repair and also look into replacing the trees with something smaller, but native to these parts, that will also provide a wind break and nature habitat. As well as being native, we would like to be looking to be able to coppice the new trees as an additional fuel source for the range in the future.

We have also now been able to dig out a new driveway to the side of the cottage and start some of the landscaping of the grounds. (It is great having friends from your daughter's school who have their own mini digger and are prepared to help you out in their spare time – well done Ritchie!)

We also managed to enlarge the soak away area at this time and now need to source some reeds or willow to finish it off. Marion's uncle, then helped by collecting some stone from the local quarry to throw down on the drive & bed down to give a firm base before being topped off.

TO BE CONTINUED.

Chapter Five

Diary of an Irish Stone Cottage Renovation Continues

Original Blog Date: Tuesday, October 5, 2010

August 2009 – August 2010.

Because of the materials we used in insulating the cottage, decorating was a relatively easy job in comparison to some of the earlier jobs. No need to use wallpaper to aid insulation, as we had a breathable lining in the 'Sasmox' boarding and all we had to do was paint the walls.

So, having had the help of family before during the building phase, we now had a family painting party to decorate the interior of the cottage; why do it yourself when you have friends and family willing to help out? The handmade doors that were hung on the bedrooms and shower/wet room were stained with a wood stain, to maintain the natural feel of the cottage. As well, leading into autumn, we decided to give the outside walls another coat of paint, just in time as it happened - or so we thought!!!!

As you might remember, last winter was one of the worst we've had in many years and the West of Ireland was no different. During November we had the wettest month we had experienced since arriving in Roscommon. Storms and floods were the order of the day, cars and property suffering in almost equal measure. At least the cottage was on a raised site, so it wasn't liable to flooding. However, along with the rain came some gale force winds off the Atlantic Ocean and combine those two elements with a sudden drop in temperature, that brought snow, ice and frost and we had conditions that would find out any weakness in the fabric of the cottage.

Unfortunately, just before Christmas, Andy's Dad died suddenly and without warning over in England and everything had to be dropped in order to travel over for the funeral and the sorting out of all the other arrangements that go with it. Because of the time of year, events dragged on into January and it was the end of the month before Andy got back to

Roscommon. By the time we were all back, the elements had taken their toll on the cottage. The render on one of the end walls had partly fallen off, as had some around the chimney and I realised then that the original sand / lime render mix was wrong, so I had some repairs to do - when the weather improved!

It's only when you're trying to juggle various different aspects of your life and trying to start your own business that you realise how time consuming each of these individual tasks can be! So, the repairs got left longer than was ideal and when I had the time, the weather usually conspired against me doing the work needed. Even so, it was eventually completed, the stable door on the porch was fitted and the light fitting in the porch sorted.

The covering top of the water well was beginning to look a little the worse for wear after the winter months, so it was decided to re-style it and the separate log store, utilising Andy's dry stone walling skills.

So here we are, up to date; the current 'to do' jobs include replacing the cracked concrete path around the cottage with gravel, to have a uniform look to the path and driveway and also to ensure the exterior paintwork is up to scratch before yearend. Finally, Marion is most insistent that we get the ground prepared for a vegetable patch for next year.

So, for now, that's it. Don't forget to leave your thoughts or comments, or contact us with any questions, if we can we will try to answer everyone.

Andy & Marion

(October 2010).

The Benefit of Hindsight and Learning

Chapter Six

Diary of an Irish Stone Cottage Renovation Revisited – Continued Development

December 2021.

A lot has happened in-between the final entry on my diary Blog pages back in October 2010 and today. Originally, I just noted things down as a personal journal to look back on in later years, or for reference if something had gone wrong or even if I was tempted to try something similar again in the future. Or maybe just to hand to our daughter in my dotage!

What I didn't realise was that people might be interested in the original journey and it was only after a nudge or two that I turned the diary into a blog post, uploaded it onto the web and almost forgot about it, that was 2009 – 2010. Three years later I was having a spring clean of my laptop and stumbled across the blog and out of curiosity decided to have a look at the viewing numbers. Over 1,500 viewings with me not doing anything to promote or advertise its existence - oh wow! I think my initial view was if I had a euro for each of those views, we could have had a nice family summer holiday somewhere. Anyway, that was when I first thought of turning the blog into an e-book and uploading it into Kindle.

That was now over eight years ago, (or eleven for the blog) and time moves on, people change, ideas change and hindsight becomes a marvellous tool if you look back and learn from those actions rather than just wish you'd done something differently, know what I mean?

Would I do it again? On your own, even with key helpers, it is a slow business, so I would say that if time is of the essence, then no, I wouldn't do it again, I would get in the professionals. However, if you have the time, energy and resources and are looking for a challenge or a reason to push your own personal boundaries further and accept the stresses, strains and pride that goes with completing a major project like this, especially with no previous construction experience, then yes, I would do it all again.

Anyway, how did we use the cottage in those years since?

One thing that I didn't cover in the blog was the impact of the bank crisis in Ireland between 2008 and 2010. As our estimated budget for the project got ever closer, it became obvious that we wouldn't be able to do some of the more adventurous and sustainable ideas we had spoken about unless a new money stream showed itself to us. I was thankful to a certain degree that we had saved a good 'wedge' of money by doing a lot of the labour ourselves or with family and friends, rather than retaining a building firm to do the work. I had taken a job in nearby Roscommon Town in 2008 in a new start up home improvement store, the money helped as we finished off the renovation and I managed to pick up bits and pieces with a staff discount in store, but again it wasn't the best time to start a new retail business and attract customers, as everyone seemed to keep a tight hold of what money they had. Sure, enough the store eventually closed and that pushed us into finding new income streams.

With the cottage renovation and decoration complete, Marion and her mother sent out a general invitation to the extended family to come and stay at the cottage after we had finished the renovation in 2010. Some did, some didn't, but what was most gratifying was that most of Marion's aunts and uncles did come along to see what we had done and reminisce over their time growing up in the cottage. In fact, more than once we would find her mother and some of the sister's sitting in front of the range gazing out of the window at the views over the Roscommon fields, talking of the old days. There is something special in watching and listening to an older generation talking about how it was and how life was totally different to today.

In April 2012 Marion's mother arranged for a 'Station Mass' to be held in the cottage, to which family, friends and neighbours were all invited to attend. For those unfamiliar with modern day rural Irish life, a Station is a Catholic Mass, which is still celebrated around Easter time in different parishioner's home's each year and gives a reason to smarten up the house to try and impress the neighbours.

The tradition dates back to the Penal Laws, (when English rulers under Oliver Cromwell and the Roundheads, also known as the Puritans, after the English Civil War during the mid- late seventeenth century, tried to force a national change of religion from Roman Catholicism to the relatively recent Protestant religion) when it was forbidden for Catholic priests to say Mass in public. To get around the problem, the Mass was often celebrated secretly in people's homes, and afterwards, those in attendance stayed on for a full day of merriment - but only after the priest had finished and taken his leave! So, in true fashion, we had a bit of a party after the Mass and Father Browne even hung around for a bite to eat and socialise with his 'flock'.

So having moved out of the cottage and set up home fairly close by to accommodate three generations; Marion's mother was now living with us, we had to decide how best to utilise the cottage and try to earn some cash from a new and innovative business undertaking and repay our bank account with some of the money we had invested in the renovation.

Marion had recently qualified as a Life and Business Coach and an obvious idea was for her to use the cottage as the base for coaching sessions with clients, being remote, away from distractions and in the middle of the Roscommon countryside; while she continued to develop her ideas into a new offering as a 'Positive Energy Coach', which she continues to practice to this day.

Andy, as mentioned before had traditional dry stone walling skills that he had learnt in Lancashire, England, (that is building stone walls without the aid of mortar or cement) before moving over to Ireland and then honed once at the cottage using the totally different local stone! So, another idea to surface was to hold 'learn the basic dry stone walling skills' weekends, to take away and use in your own gardens and homes, walls, flower beds, you name it; once you have the skills your garden is your oyster.

In addition, in 2011 and 2012 we opened the cottage up to public scrutiny during National Heritage Week, not really sure who or if anyone would want to come and see what we had achieved on our journey to date, but in the hope of gaining some positive feedback and free advertising through word of mouth in the town and its surrounds. Much to our surprise we had a very successful opening both times, with many complimentary comments such as;

*Rae from Ballybeg – "Love what you've done here.'

*Jim and Grace from the U.S. via Strokestown – "Good effort, very welcoming."

*Margaret and Tracy from Tulsk – "A wonderful, tranquil cottage."

*Mike and Melissa from Strokestown – "A lovely restoration, warm and sunny atmosphere. Well done."

*Don and Liz from Cloonmeen – Beautiful cottage, lovingly renovated. really interesting."

*Nuala and Julie from Dublin – "Thank you for opening your beautiful house to us and congrats on the wonderful results of your hard work and creativity."

*Trisha and Pat from Carrowroe – "Beautiful restored cottage, great job."

As we moved forward, our neighbour up the lane Penny had told us how she had got help for her goat farm from an organisation called WWOOF Ireland, (Worldwide Opportunities on Organic Farms, Ireland) and that once you registered on their website you could get helpers through your door to help with work around the property.

Ok so we aren't a farm, but our renovation was sustainably done, so we approached them and they said ok.

In 2014 we welcomed our first Wwoofer, Bertrand from Tours in France and he stayed for three weeks, quickly followed by Mathilde and Lauriane from France for two weeks each helping with general labouring work, while I showed them how to construct dry stone walls and they rebuilt the dividing wall between the two sections of garden, so that going forward we could start work on a fruit and vegetable area on one side and have a recreational area on the other side.

After being so lucky with our various Wwoofer helpers, we started looking at using the cottage as a holiday retreat, a peaceful home from home, offering additional extra's from some of the various skills that Marion and I had picked up, from the coaching and walling, through to 'Reiki' and 'Laughter Yoga' sessions. We started advertising the cottage on 'AirBnb' as a step back in time, with minimal modern-day conveniences such as a television and more like how Marion's grandparents would have lived back in their day.

After a slowish start, bookings started to really pick up, especially during the warmer summer months of 2015, '16 and '17, before dropping off a bit in 2018 and '19. During that time, we had almost universally positive comments about the cottage, its location and what we were offering to the wider world. Our visitors came from far and wide, not just Ireland; but from Canada, Australia, France, Denmark, the USA, French Guyana, the UK, Switzerland, New Zealand, Germany, South Africa and Iceland to name just a few.

Visits lasted between a couple of days and up to a few weeks and we got some lovely comments in return;

*James and Charissa, Australia; "Thanks for the privilege of staying in your cottage. Nice to wake up to nature and cows! Well done. Bonza mate!"

*Jesper, Denmark; "Had an excellent stay. So nice to get away from it all and just simply be. This is an absolute beautiful house and everything was grand. I loved it here and will always remember the peace and the beauty."

*David and Courtney, USA; "Don't cry because it's over, smile because it happened. (Dr Seuss)."

*Adam and Sam, Canada; "Our stay brought new meaning to the term 'Holy Cow!' How grateful we are for the pioneer style retreat. Slainte and merci!!"

*Chad, USA; "I'll be back!"

*Sharon, New Zealand; "Amazing – just what I needed. Thank you so much Marion and Andy."

*Dave and Jessica, USA; "Our time here was life changing. We'll miss the cottage! Thank you for the chance of a lifetime."

*Ronja and Deirdre, Germany; "Amazing place to be. Lovely cottage and time to relax."

*Halla and Katla, Iceland; "We had the pleasure of staying here at Connors Retreat for just a few days. Marion and Andy have really done a great job renovating the place......All in all an unforgettable experience that we most highly recommend for everyone!"

*Ana, Germany; "Peaceful and perfect, a real experience of Ireland and connecting to history. I will miss the cottage and will return!"

So, 2019 moved into 2020 and the beginnings of the Covid-19 pandemic, as we all know now, travel ground to a halt and we were unable to keep as close an eye on the cottage as we would have liked. It was beginning to show signs of wear and tear, from its continued use for one thing or another over the years and from the weather conditions that we regularly enjoy here in the West of Ireland. Unfortunately, due to the various lock-down requirements we were unable to tackle these 'fixes' as we would have liked and the cottage remained empty and unattended, for most of the year.

Towards the end of the year and out of the blue, we were asked if we would consider renting the cottage out on a long term let to a French family who were in urgent need of somewhere to stay, but within their tight budget. Having explained the situation, not having been used for most of the year and therefore cold and showing some signs of damp in places, they took it on having agreed to help with some of the work needed in return for a cheap rent.

With Morgane and Simon now in residence for more than a few weeks, we managed to once again get some heat into the cottage on a regular and continual basis, although probably the main achievement that we achieved during this time, was in putting in place some new drainage piping around the cottage to help take away the excess rain water, that had a habit of collecting at the bottom of the cottage walls causing the damp problem in one or two places.

Unfortunately, come the spring of 2021, the family decided that they would have to return to France and the cottage once again fell quiet and cold.

Chapter Seven (Summary & Conclusion)

Hindsight (can be a continued source of learning!)

December 2021

So, looking back to the start of this journey what, with hindsight would I perhaps do differently? What have we learnt about old style stone cottages, left derelict in a field to succumb to nature's ravages of time and to the local wildlife? Well, coming into this I obviously had no building or construction experience and although we were lucky in having several family members who were experienced, a lot of what I learnt came either from YouTube videos, or on the spot learning; sometimes it worked, sometimes it didn't and we've learnt through the school of hard knocks!

I suppose the first thing to mention is that the ambitious route that we took was almost inevitably more expensive than just getting a builder in to knock the building and follow our plans to rebuild it from scratch in the modern way. But that wasn't the issue here; we had decided to try and keep something from a bygone era that would be fairly recognisable to Marion's grandparents if they could return and step inside and see what we had done with 'their' cottage!

If I was to change anything from the initial prepping and weather proofing stage of the renovation, it would be how I originally approached the damp and outside render. Instead of just tackling and removing the loose patches and repairing them as I did, I would now go the whole hog and remove the whole outside render, on all of the walls and chimney stack and have a completely new watertight, but breathable lime render applied, but nevertheless one hundred per cent new. What we have found over the years, is that as patches become loose and/or fall off, they in turn allow sections next to the weakened area to become loose. It's like a 'Forth Road Bridge job' as we sometimes say, a constant fight in order to keep abreast of, when you finish you inevitably find another patch needing fixing! It would also make financial and timely sense to have done this, as once completed you wouldn't have to keep returning to fix these small patches year after year. In fact, the lesson was learnt when I had the chimney stack properly rendered the year before Covid struck and haven't had a problem with it since.

The issue we had with condensation inside the cottage when we first moved in was due to not giving it time to dry out properly after so many years of being empty and derelict and also not having enough heating options inside the cottage. Looking back now I would definitely be looking in investing in under-floor heating and either an air-to-air heat pump, or geothermal heating, (although both still in their infancy back around here when we began, so not an option for us then). By having this regular heating available, instead of just the solid fuel range, the cottage in addition to the drainage work, would not have had the intermittent problems with cold and damp like it has had over these recent years. I would also be looking at the use of heated water solar panels to maximise the availability of hot water in the cottage. I stress once again that back in 2006/7 Ireland, a lot of these technologies were still in their infancy and had a significant and prohibitive cost for such a small renovation operation like ours; but today would be much more achievable and attractive, even sometimes having the option of and benefitting from financial grants available from government backed operations like S.E.I. (Sustainable Energy Ireland).

Also, as part of the damp problem, I would have looked into improving the drainage around the cottage earlier than we did. I had started on the right track by laying a loose shingle path around the outside of the cottage, but from talking to other locals in the area found that I hadn't gone anywhere near deep or wide enough, in order to help the rain water drain away successfully from the cottage. One guy told me that I should have probably dug down about six feet and three to four feet wide before filling the trench with chipping stone. Even then, I would still have had to have put in drainage pipes in each corner of the building to aid the flow away. So, it is well worth talking to people who know the weather, the lie of the land and have at some time or other been involved with 'newbuilds' or renovation projects in the nearby area. In fact, get the basics right at the start and you save money further down the road! But as I said before, with little experience in this type of work we were learning as we went along.

The compost toilet has been something that has drawn comment from our visitors from day one, but was it the correct decision at the time? Well, the alternative was a septic tank that from time to time would have required emptying at an additional and on-going cost. It would also have had to have had planning permission from the Local Council department, again at a cost. Our decision meant no black water being moved from the cottage to a resting site, possibly contaminating the local water supply in so doing; and with the soak area that we created surrounded by native water loving trees, increased the almost certainty of only clean water returning to the original source of the underground stream. Perhaps the only issue we might review if doing this again, or with this wonderful thing called hindsight, would be the size of the unit that we actually took delivery of. Back then, we couldn't find an Irish based supplier for what we needed, we couldn't walk into a showroom and physically look at or touch a toilet unit, and we were restricted to what we could or couldn't see online. The toilet we eventually took possession of came from Canada, suitable for mountain / weekend North American lodges according to the brochure, so we thought it would be great. The only problem was its size in relation to its allocated space in a re-designed traditional Irish stone cottage; it dominated the shower/wet room, something that we as occupants now find much easier to work around, but initially certainly a problem. But all said and done, I still think that the compost toilet was the right option for us then and still is today, especially from an ecological perspective.

One of the simpler fixes that I was able to do from time to time, was the use of a chimney cowl atop the chimney pot, to help protect the range from unnecessary water damage. The problem we have here in the West of Ireland however is the number of storms that seem to come in towards us straight from the Atlantic Ocean, with strong winds that tend to batter whatever cowl we put up. I think in the fourteen odd years since we started, I have put up four different styles of cowl so far with each one being battered into submission by the elements or not allowing enough draw and smoke escaping into the cottage instead of out. The search is still on for a reliable, strong cowl to combat the Irish weather.

We made it our mission to try and keep everything as sustainable and eco-friendly as possible from the outset of this journey, but one of the items that has frustrated me are the fascia boards under the roof around the cottage. I put in wooden boards, knowing that I would probably have to treat them from one year to the next. It's not a difficult job, just time consuming and waiting on some good weather in order to complete it. Should I perhaps have used plastic boards; put them up and forget about them? To be honest, while it would be easier; in order to stay true to our intentions we did the right thing with the wooden boards.

There are always other small problems that arise from time to time, like in any home, not just a renovation, but I won't bore you with those recollections here.

So that's it, a catch up on our adventure, we hope that you enjoyed reading about our journey, it's not for everyone I know, but if you are thinking of doing a similar renovation project, I hope we have given you some ideas, observations and thoughts to ponder on as you take on your own personal adventure.

Thank you for your time and we hope that we have been able to help you in some small way.

Marion and Andy (February, 2022).

Printed in Great Britain
by Amazon

36201960R00050